Ang

C

Collection

Poems of Highland Life

With a foreword by
IAIN CRICHTON SMITH

Northern Books
from Famedram
www.northernbooks.co.uk

ISBN 0 905489 65 9
© 2001 Famedram Publishers Ltd AB41 9EA
Printed in Hungary

Foreword
by the late Iain Crichton Smith

I FIRST got to know Angus Macintyre because as a teacher in Oban High School I had come into contact with his sons. As is well known, not only is he himself a brilliant man, but he is also the father of brilliant sons one of whom, Lorn, is a poet and novelist and another, Angus, a quite outstanding logician of international reputation and probably the possessor of the most incisive mind that I have encountered in teaching. I mention this because the Bible says that by their fruits you shall know them.

I have been re-reading the poems which are to form this collection. Naturally I knew many of them before. Like the ballads, they are on the lips of the people, and certainly Angus Macintyre has a wider audience than many avant-garde poets have. It is an audience which appreciates the events of the daily routine and which recognises in his work the world in which it lives.

It is an audience that has 'The Politician' as part of its myth, and which has attended the Mod and the Oban Games. It reacts positively to the obvious love of the Highlands which breathes through the poems and also to the humour and the skill which all of them show. These are exactly the kinds of poems which that audience would write if it had the ability.

It is not an easy thing to write as humorously as this, and to have such an appeal. It requires keen observation and the ability to juxtapose the old and the new. It sees not only the old bodach and the old cailleach, but also the guitar-playing long haired son who competes with his father's bagpipes. It sees the meeting of two worlds, but it does not despair of this meeting.

If there is praise of shinty, there is also understanding of the high-heeled Glasgow girls. The world of tourism is seen with affection. But so also is the world of a loved and ancient landscape. In these rhythms one hears the echoes of earlier poets, but they are none the worse for that. It is not a mocking voice that one hears, nor is it scathing or bitter.

If I were to pick my favourite from these poems I would pick 'Lady Somesing's Lover' which I think is very fine and very funny. Anyone who thinks he could have written it should try. For Angus Macintyre has that essential gift for this kind of poetry – he never writes down to his audience. He is able to put himself into the minds of his characters and he understands them. He never patronises and this is more difficult than it looks.

Any Highlander will recognise in these poems the world in which he lives, its gentleness and its fantasies. It is a world of memories and of shrewd insight. The mind behind these poems is keen and witty and humane, and it is to these qualities that audiences have responded. There are many poets who might wish that they too could have such a direct and immediate impact.

I must say that seeing these poems in bulk I have been even more impressed than I was before. The skill is constant. The punch lines would make many comedians green with envy. I am sure that the book will be something of a best seller, and deservedly so. I look forward to seeing the poems in print and possessing the book. For not only will it have poetic interest, but in years to come it will form a memorial to those events that moved us and made us laugh when we were living in the Highlands at a particular moment in time.

IAIN CRICHTON SMITH
Oban, May 1975

Letter from the Glen

Dear Donal', how're you keepin'?
It's your mother hopes you're fine;
The others all are sleepin',
So I thought I'd drop a line.

This pen near drives me batchy –
A new word that, for me –
The nib is awful scratchy,
Since the point is all squee-gee.

The writin's no chust flowin',
An' my letter's maybe dull,
But I thought you should be knowin'
What's goin' on in Mull.

McKenzie, with the taxi
Is fair down in the dumps,
His yowes have got the braxy,
An' his Cailleach's¹ got the mumps.

He says he's nearly screwy,
An' he swears he canna sleep,
For, as he told wee Hughie,
"I can't replace the sheep".

His Cailleach's no a worry,
An' he doesn't care wan jot;
Tho' he says he wouldn't hurry,
A new one's easy got.

Your gran'pa, the old rascal,
Has brought great shame on me,
Went off with Chon MacAskill
On a most outrageous spree.

He sold a stirk last Monday,
– Och, this will make you wince,
For, Donal', now it's Sunday,
An' we haven't seen him since.

But, M'eudail, we've been hearin'
A thing of deep disgrace,
An' true it is, I'm fearin',
Tho' truth is hard to face.

The postman told your father,
Who raged and clenched his fist,
"The Bodach's up in Dervaig
With MacAskill – doin' the Twist."

An' granny told your sister,
"My girl, it's true, I'm sure,
He was aye the *biggest twister*
From Dervaig to Craignure."

You'll know your Uncle Bertie
Is marrying Cheanie Robb,
They've been going since nineteen-thirty
So they didn't rush the job.

I hope they'll be agreein'
An' I'm sure they'll get on fine,
But I don't sink we'll be seein'
Many nappies on the line.

Now, Donald, in the city,
Be sure you do not flirt,
Stay faithful to wee Kitty,
An' see an' change your shirt.

Beware of sinful people,
Who'll leave you in the lurch,
Let your landmark be a steeple,
An' your refuge be a Church.

An' Donald, write a letter,
To give me all your news,
By then we'll all feel better,
Wis Gran'pa off the booze.

P.S. He's back, the old rascal,
As cocky as can be,
Himself and Chon MacAskill,
Wis a 'snifter just for me.

I'm wild, as are your brothers,
An' I will not take his part,
But a man who thinks of others
Is a gentleman at heart.

[1] Gaelic for *old woman*

Islay Cheese

(Whose import into Italy was banned several years ago because of its alleged aphrodisiac qualities)

You Highland women I implore
Upon my bended knees,
Please do not eat one morsel more
Of that awful Islay Cheese.

No more the 'Tallies' smack their lips
O'er mounds of Macaroni;
They are not moved by fish and chips,
It's Islay Cheese for Tony.

Vincente Dopi – ninety-two –
Well past all thoughts of fun –
Ate half a pound and what'd he do,
But go and squeeze a nun.

The Pope has cried, "Enough, enough,
Away with this love potion,
The wild and wanton Islay stuff,
That puts them in the notion.

I banned the Pill – a sinful curse –
– I felt their morals soar –
And now there comes a thing far worse,
This menace from Bowmore."

Luigi Silli – eighty-four –
And never termed a flirt
Went tearing out his own back door,
Chasing a mini skirt.

An old and shaking Genoese,
His pension was collectin',
Ate just one bite of Islay Cheese,
And now his wife's expectin'.

He chews a chunk and softly sighs,
"How I love this glorious Cheesa,"
Looks up aloft and loudly cries,
"Get up them stairs, Teresa."

The old wife prays upon her knees,
"Oh Lord, restrain his sallies,
And from this awful Islay Cheese,
Protect us poor old Tallies."

Memories of Mull

Do you remember, brother, those times of long ago,
When the yacht's white sails were gleaming
In the red sun's afterglow,
And the Aros Woods are greening
Where the hawthorn lay like snow?

And are you mindin' brother, the sun on
    Loch-na-Keal,
The great dark cliffs of Gribun, and the West
    Wind's salty feel;
High summer in Glen Bellart, where the
    endless Moorlands start,
And the winding road to Dervaig that's
    tangled round my heart?

The grim, gaunt Keep of Duart, 'neath storm
    clouds darkly massed
Maintaining wary vigil as the long dark ages
    passed;
The sunlit bays of summer, cloud shadow on
    the hills
And the tinkle, tinkle of the crystal Island
    rills.

The peat smoke curling, lazy, in the heather
    scented moon,
And the bare foot children happy in the day
    that passed too soon;
In the woods of Killiechronan, bird-song at
    close of day,
And the creaming, frothing breakers,
    streaming into Fishnish Bay.

Salen, lying dreaming in the sleepy August
    haze,
And the bracken turning yellow in the
    mellow Autumn days;
Loch Uisk, the pines reflecting in the long
    low evening light,
Bunessan's lamp-lit windows, in the witching
    Island night.

The green translucent water, and the sunlight
    on the sand,
The holy peace that blesses Iona's hallowed
    strand;
Soft fluted notes at even', of a curlew on
    the shore,
Loch Baa in summer twilight, or moonlight
    on Ben More.

And it's back to Tobermory with the
     moonlight on the Bay,
Or the swan-white yachts a-shining on a
     sunlit Summer's day;
Tho' those lovely scenes keep fading like
     flowerlets in the grass,
The kindness of the Island folks for me will
     never pass.

The mazy road that wanders by Calgary's
     white sand,
Torloisk and Ulva Ferry, that lone and lovely
     land;
Or the bonny way that's wending by lochan,
     sea and moor,
From Fionnphort to Uisgean, Lochbuie to
     Craignure.

And let us sing together the Gaelic songs
     we sung
In Clachan and in sheiling, in the days when
     we were young;
Remembering the old folks, the stock from
     which we grew,
The dear folks, the good folks, the kind an
     the true.

From the faded blooms of mem'ry,
    blossoms that I cull
Smell sweet of golden summers, of happy
    days in Mull;
I cherish them and keep them and, friends,
    I pray of you
To homeland, Friends, and Language, keep
    ever staunchly true.

Lady Somesing's Lover

Old Sandy puffed his ancient briar
As one more puff he took,
Chust there beside the red peat-fire,
And told me of *The Book*.

"An awful thing to print an' bind,
– A Penguin on the cover –
Its name has somehow slipped my mind,
But it's Lady Somesing's Lover.

You know, to read this awful book
Was not my heart's desire;
I chust had one wee ling'ring look
While Morag cleaned the byre.

Because I neffer had the chance,
For even while in bed,
She sat like someone in a trance
And read, and read and read.

You'll neffer know a woman's quirks,
Tho' you are old and sage;
She chust sat there all grins and smirks
An' turned another page.

No work was done, no food she took,
No preakfast bacon fried;
She chust sat there wiss that damn book
An' smiled an' gasped an' sighed.

She rose at last to clean the byre,
An' Chon, my chance I took;
I sat down here beside the fire
An' keeked inside the book.

Now only once I heard such words –
Wee short ones, Chon, you know,
Wass the time my Uncle proke his nose
On the day of Salen Show.

I've been gamekeeping all my life,
But sure as kestrels hover,
I neffer wass a lucky man
Like Lady Somesing's Lover.

For fifty years I roamed Ben More
An' shot o'er moor and butt,
But, Chon, it leaves me wild an' sore
To read of that wee hut.

"Do this, do that, go here, go there,"
According to their mood,
But no lady came to visit me
In my bothy in the wood.

For, Chon, you see it makes me sob,
That I was born too soon;
This fellow did not have a job,
It wass a Honeymoon.

An' now this house is all to pot
For Morag drives me frantic;
She says "You're chust a great beeg clot,
So dull an' unromantic.

You maybe know the glen and wood,
An' haunts of Golden Plover,
But you neffer were wan half so good,
As Lady Somesing's Lover."

She says, "Had I but got the chance,
By Chove I would not tarry;
I wouldn't cast you wan wee glance,
It's yon Cave-Man I'd marry."

"For neffer wance in all your life,
In sunshine or in shower,
Did *you* gather posies for your wife,
To deck me in my bower."

In 1941 The Politician, with a huge cargo of whisky aboard, foundered off the Island of Barra in the Outer Hebrides. Sir Compton MacKenzie immortalised the hilarious incidents that followed, in his famous "Whisky Galore": Novelists are traditionally permitted much licence and why not Rhymers, too?

"The Politician"

"Och, times are hard in Barra",
You'll hear the Bodachs[1] cry,
"No food to feed a sparra,
An' effery bottle dry".

Old men, once fresh an' frisky,
So full of ploy and play,
Dropped dead for want of whisky,
– The plessed Uisque-bae.

Now, the dusty dry Sahara
Iss a bare an' barren land,
But the drought that year in Barra
Wass more than man could stand.

Aye, life was hard an' cruel,
And days were long an' sad,
When the strongest drink wass gruel
An' the war wass goin' bad.

A cleffer man, Old Hector,
An' wise the words he said,
"Wisout the barley's nectar
A man iss better dead."

But strange the ways of Heaven,
When men in darkness grope;
Each sorrow has its leaven,
Each tragedy its hope.

The great Ship, Politician,
Her hold stocked high wis grog,
Steamed proudly past the Island,
An' foundered in the fog.

A case was rent assunder,
Twelve bottles came to grief,
When the Barra surf, like thunder,
Came pounding on the Reef.

And then the scent of nectar
Came on the wild wind's breath,
"I smell it", screamed Old Hector,
"It's whisky – sure as death"

He yelled out, "Kirsty, Kirsty,
Bring down my oilskin coat;
No more will we be thirsty,
Salvation's in that boat".

Tho' thirst her tongue had blistered,
Old Kitsty forced a laugh;
"I'm comin' too" she whispered,
"It's me that needs a half"[2]

Now, Chon MacNeill wass dying;
The death that's far the worst;
No end so sad an' tryin'
As the fatal pangs of thirst.

For weeks he had been lying,
Wisout a sign of life,
An' all the neighbours crying
For his nearly widowed wife.

He sobbed, "I am delivered,
From torture I am free",
As his nostrils flared an' quivered
In the glory from the Sea.

He shook chust like an aspen
The man they though was dead,
An' sighin', gulpin', gaspin',
He vaulted out of bed.

Barefooted, in his nightie,
He slipped from out their reach,
Wis steps bose long an' mighty
He headed for the beach.

Now, Sarah Chane MacKinnon,
– A lady through an' through,
Wass chust a wee bit partial
To a drop of Mountain Dew.

She brooded at the ingle,
Her form all old an' bent,
When her blood began to tingle
At a well-remembered scent.

Wan sniff an' she wass rising,
Two sniffs an' straight outside,
Where odours appetising
Were blowing from the tide.

By chove, she went full throttle
Across the Barra turf,
When she heard a tinkling bottle,
In the thunder of the surf.

She ran, but so did others,
Och hundreds, maybe more,
As Uncles, cousins, brothers,
Stampeded for the shore.

The boats went gaily dashing
Across the crested wave;
The long oars dipping, splashing
To their Aladdin's cave.

They climbed aboard the liner,
The halt, the lame, the old,
No Vikings e'er were finer,
No Pirates half so bold.

They peered wis anzious faces,
Within the gaping hold,
An' saw a thousand cases,
Of precious, liquid gold.

"A shame, A shame," cried Kirsty,
"It iss an act of God,
Chust think of Barra, thirsty,
An' all this goin' abroad".

Och, the Ceilidhs, och, the pleasure,
Oh the choy in Castle*bay,*
As the gurglin', golden treasure
Chased the cares of war away.

Och, the bottles that were hidden,
Buried deep beneath the croft;
Oh, the cases in the midden,
Och, the choy up in the loft.

Who would heed an air-raid warning,
Who would hide himself in fright?
Wis a tumbler in the morning
An' a bumper late at night.

An' Barra boys, hard-fighting
On sea and ocean wide,
Deserved their wee bit parcel
Wis glook, glook, glook inside.

Old Hector cried, "We're winning,
The fact is plain to me,
This night is the beginning
Of victory at sea."

He swigged another Chug-full,
An' happily he sighed,
"The Germans sure have had it,
Now Barra's fortified".

"A Slainte[3] now for Churchill,
His name I proudly call,
But the .Barra Politician
Is the greatest of them all."

[1] Gaelic for *old men*
[2] A glass of whisky
[3] Gaelic for *good health*

The Old Game

The shinty game is failing
Throughout the Northern Land
Whilst we stand here, bewailing,
And raise no helping hand.

Let Gaels all stand together,
As steadfast as the Bens,
To see that stick on leather
Keeps echoing in our glens.

At the dying peats I'm sitting,
And back from days of yore
Come sounds of crisp, clean hitting,
The cheers, the clever score.

The jousting and the swinging,
The subtle, silken slip
From men, whose way of winning
Despised the hack and trip.

An' the great names I am minding
Flood back from yester year;
The list's too long, I'm finding,
To put them all down here.

From Oban up to Spean,
From Newtonmore to Kyles,
Came stalwarts, all worth seein'
Well skilled in shinty's wiles.

Strong men from far Lochaber,
All upright, broad and tall;
With strength to toss a caber,
Or hit a pitch-length ball.

Fleet-footed men from Furnace,
And lnveraray Town,
Went North to Ballachullish
To throw the gauntlet down.

A challenge that was taken,
In battles fierce to see,
When valiant hearts were shaken
On the famous *Jubilee*.[1]

Kingussie, cute an' cunning,
Clever, sharp an' slick
Were always in the running,
Old Maestros of the stick.

And cheering on the players,
The Bodachs let it rip,
Wi' words no' found in prayers –
– An' "snifters" at their hip.

It wass not there for boozin',
For that was neffer done;
To comfort you when losin'
And cheer you when you won.

Tho' you seldom had the notion,
You sometimes made so bold,
As to swig an extra potion,
In case you got the cold.

No man of rightful thinking
Would overdo *"The stuff"*
For he might get keen on drinking,
An' wan bottle wass enough.

No yelling an' no shouting,
No beer-cans on the sward;
Nor "Polis" busy clouting,
– For that we thank the Lord.

Just skill an' manly striving
In shinty's ancient arts,
That kept the old game thriving,
And gladdened Highland hearts.

All storms the Game will weather,
Both strong an' proud will stand,
If brave we fight together
Throughout this Bonnie Land.

To keep our shinty living,
With hand an' heart engage;
Start working and start giving
To save our heritage!

[1] Jubilee Park at Ballachulish

Conversation at Tobermory Pier, June 1959

The Bodach[1] leaned against the pier,
With red and angry eye,
And said to me "It's very clear,
There's madmen loose in Skye".

"They've got a boat, the very best,
Renowned both near and far,
Beloved of folks in all the west,
The Dear Old 'Lochinvar'".

"For fifty years in surge and swell,
Her trim and sturdy hull,
Brought friends and food – aye, drink as well,
To grateful folks in Mull".

"Now this Dame Flora screams in pain,
– You know what women are –
And urges on My Lords MacBrayne
To scrap the 'Lochinvar'".

"An' listen man, I'm just as sure,
As my name's Chon MacKay,
What's good enough for Craignure²
Is far too good for Skye".

"The Tourist Trade will surely fail".
Is now her angry cry,
For visitors, they will not sail
Across the sea to Skye".

"Her Clansmen, loyal, proud an' staunch.
Join in the fume and fret;
It makes me smile – my wee bit launch
Could carry all they'll get."

"You do not need much schoolin',
– I'm certain on this score –
To know the bare, bleak Cuillin
Can never match Ben More".

"The great seas number seven,
And I've sailed them in my day –
But there's no place nearer Heaven,
Than Tobermory Bay".

"Now Captain Black and all his crew,
For manners were renowned,
And glad I am to say to you,
They are not Skyeward bound".

"For listen, man, the truth let's face,
However hard they'd try.
They may have lost their Christian grace,
Out there in Heathen Skye".

"You may be somewhat chary,
But hear the truth from me,
It seems Cunard's Queen Mary,
Is wanted in Portree".

For Skye, Dame Flora's zealous,
But I think it's got her goat,
And left her mad an' jealous,
To get Mull's discarded boat."

[1] Gaelic for *old man*
[2] Pronounced Craig-en-nure

Peace in the Sheiling

You can picture the elation
When our Donald wrote the note,
'I am coming on vacation,
You can meet me at the boat.'

'My music I'll be bringin',
To give you all a tune,
Yes, music hot an' swingin',
Ta-ta then, see you soon.'

The boat came swiftly steamin',
An' docked so trim and neat,
While we bose stood there, all beamin',
Our piper-son to greet.

We saw old Eachen's Ronald,
An' towrists by the score
But our braw, kilted Donald,
He didn't step ashore.

It was a sad poseetion,
As I wiped the salty tear,
When a fearful appareetion
Came slinkin' up the Pier.

A girl wis winkle-pickers,
An' jeans so tight an' thin,
Of flimsy stuff like knickers,
An' hair that reached her chin.

Across her shoulders, swingin',
Was strapped a long guitar,
An a cissie voice came ringin'
"Say folks, *so there you are.*"

My Bodach's face went ashen,
– A sight to grieve an' vex
As he said wis white-hot passion,
"Why haff you changed your sex?"

"You're chust a great, beeg Cissie,
In that outlandish rig;
So, first of all, *get busy,*
Pull off that bloody wig."

That raised our Donal's gander,
He tossed his foot-long hair,
An' yelled, "A salamander
You'll get, you Hielan' Square."

We're here now in the sheiling,
An' peace has flown afar,
My nerves an' senses reeling,
Wis the din of that guitar.

For Donal' keeps on strummin'
All day an' night as well,
An' in my ears is drummin'
The melody of hell.

My Bodach's hand was itchin',
To shake his tangled hair,
So I moved him from the kitchen
An' sent him up the stair.

But there his pipes are skirlin',
An' I've really got the gripes,
Wis' my splittin' head all whirlin'
At the twangin' an' the pipes.

The Bodach's Gaelic swearin'
Gives me such a shock,
But Donal's quite uncarin',
Yells, "ROCK, BABY, ROCK."

To me this is a blunder,
You know what pipers are,
Himself he blows like thunder,
To drown that damned guitar.

Wan week has passed in sorrow,
This din will never cease,
So I'm clearin' off tomorrow,
For Glasgow, *to get peace*.

The Jubilee Mod at Oban
October 1953

Och, can you point the bottom
Of a bottle to the sky,
Or thunder out a "slainte"[1]
To the nectar of the rye?

And if you wave a tartan
Above your brawny knee,
You surely were in Oban
In the year of Choobilee.

Now, Hector John MacTavish,
His Uncle Dan and me
All boarded a beeg liner
At Scarinish in Tiree.

My mother dabbed her hankie
To wipe away the tears,
'Twas the first time we'd been parted
In all my seexty years.

"Ochone", her voice called, "Sandy",
Above the engine's noise,
"You'll watch those girls in Oban,
They say they're daft for boys."

An' then across the gangway,
A final word I flung,
"Yes, Mammy, I'll be careful,
I'm a fly one, Tho' I'm *young*,"

We sailed across the Ocean
To Bonnie Oban Bay,
And there was the beeg city,
Lit up as bright as day.

Och, scared wass I and shaking,
But Hector took my hand,
And brave we chumped together,
On this Strange, foreign land.

Oh, the bustle, the commotion,
Och, the chostling an' the throng;
Then, like the voice of Angels,
I heard a Gaelic song.

An' choy wass mine in Oban,
As my troubles slipped away,
When the strains of "Rory's Wedding",
Were wafted o'er the bay.

The tartans of Clanranald,
MacKenzie an' MacRae,
MacDougall and MacVarish
Were there in proud array.

And effery man around us,
Fron Benderloch to Kyle,
Wass talking in the Gaelic,
– The only tongue worse-while.

An' Och, the "Kimmer a ha oos"[2]
That fell from effery lip,
An' effery man that spoke them
Had a wee bulge at his hip.

Then a friendly man came forward,
Who put us in a car,
That rushed us to our quarters,
In a *bed-room next the bar.*

An' Hector Chon MacTavish,
He whispered low to me,
"I will not care wan docken,
If I neffer see Tiree."

Och, the whisky flowin' golden,
Wis story and wis song,
The hoochin' an' the birlin
At the Ceilidhs, lastin' long.

But, Oh the girls in Oban
Fair stole the heart of me;
There neffer wass their equal
At Scarinish in Tiree.

An' one, wis kilt an leepstick,
Sat down upon my knee,
An' wheespered, "Sandy, Maydull,[3]
You're chust the boy for me.

Cried she, "Oh, what a feegure,
An' a beaver like a goat's,
How I love your knobbly kneecaps,
An' your sporran, full of notes."

When I heard her mention money,
I sought that I wass tricked,
For my father, wance in Glasgow,
Had got his sporran picked.

But she cried, "Don't look so frightened,
You cuddly hunk of honey,
It's yourself *I'm* wantin', Sandy,
To the devil wis your money."

I knew then that she loved me,
An' my heart near burst wiss joy,
So I smacked her on the leepstick,
And she whispered, "Boy, oh, Boy."

Sobbed she, "You paralyse me,"
As she stroked my hairy cheek,
"You great beeg Valentino,
My desert island sheik."

Said she, "I'm sick of Oban,
I'll voyage o'er the sea,
To settle wiss you, Sandy,
On the Island of Tiree."

So I wired to my mother,
"Chust air the double bed,
Because myself an' Flora,
Are going to be wed."

And when we got to Scarinish
My mother's wrath had thawed,
For Flora wore the medal,
She had won at Oban Mod.

1 Pronounced as *slante* – Gaelic for *good health*
2 Spelled phonetically – Gaelic salutation
3 Spelled phonetically – Gaelic for *darling*

The Games

Och, the traffic that was flowin'
Of Bodachs[1] and their Dames,
And effery one wass goin'
To Tobermory Games.

Old Cailleachs[2] from Lochaline,
– MacGilvrays and MacVicars –
Young bloods from Sunart's Salen
Complete with winkle pickers.

The wee "Lochbuie" kept churnin',
Wis her o'ercrowded hull,
An' all those sousands burnin'
To set their feet in Mull.

Of course, you'll all be knowin'
Myself wass in the van,
Wis Erchie from Kilchoan,
– A brave an' sirsty man.

An' Sandy, down from Corran,
– A lad to take a trick –
Wis a "jeelack"[3] in his sporran,
In case we got sea-sick.

We landed, us blood brothers,
Us boys who'd travelled far,
Said "ta-ta" to the others
An' headed for the bar.

Och, the folks that I wass seein'
Old friends so dear to me.
Big Lachie from Strontian,
And Murdo from Tiree.

There's choy when friends are meetin'
An' ne'er wan moment dull,
As worldly cares go fleetin'
On Games Day, there in Mull.

An' such a proud procession
Was marchin' up and down;
When all the skirlin' pipers
Brought music to the town.

Then a bodach wis a shoogle
Came lurchin' in my track.
Said I, "How-do, MacDougall?"
And sumped him on the back.

Cried he in icy greeting,
"MacDougall I am not.
Methinks that I am meeting
A proper Hielan' clot."

Said I, "My friend, I'm sorry,
But chust amends I'll make.
I'm strange to Tobermory,
And I took you for a mistake."

Now, a bowly man from Dervaig
Wass cheerin' on the Band.
But clappin's no so easy
Wis a screw-top in your hand.

A man from far Tiroran
Chust nearly got his harp,
When hc reelcd an' took a header
In front of Jimmy Sharp.

But Jimmy, aye so happy,
A man to heal a rift,
Said, "Mind your step, old chappie"
Then gave the guy a lift.

A crofter from Bunessan
Wis music on his lips
Bawled out "An t-Eilean Muileach"
In between the sips.

Then up to me came runnin'
An almost breathless Miss
Who sighed, "Please tell me, Mister,
Chust where the Toilet iss?"

Now folks, here was a poser,
To set my mind askew,
So I asked her, "Tell me, lassie,
Are her funnels red or blue?"

She gasps and sadly mutters,
"Please say it isn't true,
That the Muileachs⁴ all are nutters,
Putting funnels on a Loo."

Said I, severe an' savage,
"A raspberry to you,
You asked about the Toilet,
You said nossing of the Loo."

Bad temper she wass showin'
But on such a busy day,
How could I be knowin'
Effery Vessel in the Bay?

A respite from your labours,
A time of fun and laughs;
The place to greet your neighbours,
In hearty 'Slainte-Vahs'[5].

[1] Gaelic for *old men*
[2] Gaelic for *old women*
[3] Gill of whisky
[4] Natives of Mull
[5] Phonetic Gaelic for *good health*

The Baby Sitter

I'm seventy-two and no' been wed,
– My tale is one of sorrow –
Tho' Dervaig-born and Dervaig-bred
I'm clearin' out tomorrow.

My nerves are gone, my health's away;
No wonder, folks, I'm bitter;
It happened just one week today,
When I was Baby-Sitter.

"We're goin' out," the neighbour said,
"The kids just love you, Sandy,
You sit an' read – they'll go to bed,
Och, man, you'll manage dandy."

She poured a dram, and left the glass,
"You'll take it when you're weary,
You'll never feel the evening pass,
The kids will keep you cheery."

Away she went, an' on my lap,
All smiles was Baby Aggie,
Till Willie rose an' gi'ed a slap
That felled his sister Maggie.

But Maggie's up before the bell,
– A game one, that wee filly –
Lets out a most unearthly yell,
And tears right into Wullie.

Wee Aggie clucked in deep delight
Wi' many a childish "cooey",
As Wullie ducked a snakin right,
That floored his brother, Hughie.

But Hughie wasna' easy dumped,
– A fly boy that, an' frisky –
His brother's lug he soundly thumped,
Swung round and couped[2] ma whisky.

It was the end – I yelled, "Look see
Cut out them skelps an' bashes",
When Aggie shot right off my knee,
An' landed in the ashes.

All bedlam rose, a clout I got,
From yellin', clawin' Maggie,
"Ye've done it now, you Hielan' clot,
Ye've murdered poor wee Aggie."

Although I'm old, I'm powerful built,
An' modern are ma views,
But, sad to say, beneath ma kilt,
I hadna worn ma trews.

Amid the din of shrieks an' wails,
One brat yelled out, "We've got 'im"
As a dirty foot, with sharp toenails,
Collided with ma bottom.

It's cash that counts to ease the way,
In bribes I lost ma pension;
"Now children, not one word you'll say,
To Mammy, not a mention."

Aye, home she came at midnight hour,
An' round the door was peeping,
To see the whole Satanic shower,
Like angels, soundly sleeping.

She shook ma hand, she kissed ma cheek,
Beamed fond upon her litter,
"I'm for the pictures, Thursday week,
An' you're ma Baby-Sitter."

She's 'had it', folks, I'll no' be there,
I'm off without a trace,
Tho' Daniel braved the lions' lair,
He hadna cubs to face.

[1] Spilled

Come to Tobermory
(Preferably at wance)

Now, you'll be welcome always, no matter how
    you're built,
An' be you in Bikini or gallant Highland kilt;
You can stroll along the Main Street, or wander
    o'er the moors,
An' ever do some smooching wi' the girls from
    Mainland Tours;
By chove, and they are sizzlers, these smashin'
    Glesca flirts,

Wi' their winkin' at the fellas and their dinkie
    mini-skirts;
Their men folks all are missin', but we know
    where they are,
They're downin' brimmin' glasses within the
    nearest bar,
An' buyin' pints for Greybeard, who pays for
    welcome cheer,
By romancin' on the Galleon between his swigs
    of beer.

"Och, Chentlemen, I swear it, with those two
    eyes I saw
A man wance catch a lobster wis a doubloon in
    its claw,

55

An' myself an' wee MacVicar in a boat wan
     Hogmanay
Bose saw a Spanish Galleon come sailin' in
     the Bay,

An' standin' in the wheelhouse wass a Spaniard,
     clear as clear.
Wis 'Florencia' on his bonnet and a gold ring in
     his ear;
We rowed up hard beside her, bose hopin' for
     some grog,
But the damn thing kept on sailin' an' vanished
     in the fog;
We rushed into this taproom to break the
     ghastly news,
But, Och, there's no convincin' men, whose
     only thought is booze.

Some folks will not believe that the Treasure's
     in the Bay,
But to all such foolish doubters this Gospel
     truth I'll say,
"The natives did not take it, an' the reason's
     simple, man,
The bars will not take doubloons, so such gold's
     no' worth a damn."

You can attend the Ceilidhs, if that, Sir, be
   your wish,
You can buy a raffle ticket an' maybe win a fish,
An', Och, it's glorious knowin' when the ticket
   you have bought,
That the salmon you'll be winnin' has been
   legally caught
For all the decent people we would not try
   to gull,
But a salmon caught all legal is ferry rare in Mull.

You need not bring your brolly, for rain we
   seldom get,
You may get burned with sunlight, but man you
   won't get wet,
You will not need much money, for hear the
   truth from me,
The supper, bed and breakfast are practically free.

Now you have read my message, if you think
   that it's untrue
Please hurry to your Doctor – there is somesing
   wrong wis you.

The Sale of The Lochearn to the Greeks, Summer 1964

In Cyprus all these cunning Greeks
Have put us on the rack,
And the simple British turned both cheeks,
But now, we've paid them back.

MacBraynes, as effrey Muileach[1] knows,
In guile have naught to learn,
Have slipped the Greeks a lethal dose,
And sold them **The Lochearn.**

That awful boat their hearts will break,
Of that, my man, I'm sure;
You think I lie, then heaven's sake,
Chust ask them at Craignure.

To Cyprus she's to carry food,
To feed the hungry Greeks;
I hope their constitution's good,
For they're going to starve for weeks.

The year is nineteen sixty-four,
And sure as I'm alive;
If *now* she sails for Grecian shore,
She'll be there in sixty-five.

This man, Makarios, black as sin,
Has still a lot to learn,
If he thinks a Country e'er can win,
That sails the old **Lochearn.**

Now, vicious gossip gives me pain –
– These whispers in the dark –
But I heard the Turks have paid MacBrayne,
To sell them **Noah's Ark.**

For tho' Makarios shows his teeth,
My Lords MacBrayne are smarter,
And the Turks are giving Mr Leith[2]
The Order of the Garter.

The President will kiss both cheeks,
And bless him for the hull,
That broke the spirit of the Greeks,
Like it did to us in Mull.

[1] Native of Mull
[2] MacBrayne's General Manager

Nostalgia

The honey-scented, dew-wet flowers,
That made the air so sweet;
The stillness of the gloaming hours
And the burnie at my feet,
The corncrake's rasp in the meadow grass
And the witching Highland moon;
Why did such joy so swiftly pass,
Oh why did it go so soon?

The peat-flame flickers and fades and dies,
Grotesque on the bothy wall;
The dusk is filled with seabirds' cries
And the curlew's fluted call;
But I heed them not, for my memory strays
Far back to the time lang syne;
To the golden, fleeting summer days,
When the world was fair and fine,
And the simple joys were all our need,
In the happy, Highland glen,
When friends, long-made, were friends indeed,
Steadfast as Cruachan Ben.
This was my land, my bonny land,

Beloved, dear to me;
Each rocky shore, each silver strand,
Laved by the sunlit sea.
Each corry on the snowy Ben,
The gorse in yellow blaze,
The burnie chuckling in the glen,
Enchanted boyhood days.

I cannot see, my eyes are old,
The brae is steep and sore,
But richer far than miser's gold,
The memories that I store.
Within my heart I hold and keep,
For now and evermore,
Sweet mem'ries of the friends who sleep
Far, far on Etive's shore;
And the Awe keeps purling in my ears,
As its limpid waters run
Down, down the valley of my years
To Loch Etive in the sun.
Oh, blessed me, Oh, happy man,
Of Heaven's favoured band,
To pass my joyous mortal span
In that sweet bonnie land.